Dickens' Children

A Play

Charles Dickens and Nick Warburton

A SAMUEL FRENCH ACTING EDITION

SAMUEL FRENCH

FOUNDED 1830

SAMUELFRENCH-LONDON.CO.UK
SAMUELFRENCH.COM

DICKENS' CHILDREN

First performed by Bawds at Michaelhouse in Cambridge on
16th July 2004 with the following cast:

James Dowson
Tricia Peroni
Guy Holmes
Rosemary Eason
Ken Eason
Suzi Turton
Martin Woodruff

Directed by Nick Warburton
Technical Director Richard Peroni

CHARACTERS

Charles Dickens: plays **Pip, Kenwigs Child, David Copperfield, Jo, Smike**

Actor One: plays **Mrs Kenwigs, Mrs Jellyby, Peggotty, Mrs Squeers**

Actor Two: plays **Magwitch, Kenwigs Child, Jellyby Child, Mr Squeers**

Actor Three: plays **Mr Lillyvick, Mr Kenge, Jellyby Child, Barkis, Waiter, Cobbey (Boy)**

Actor Four: plays **Mr Pumblechook, Miss Petowker, Mr Guppy, Allan Woodcourt, Nicholas Nickleby, Boy**

Actor Five: plays **Estella, Morleena Kenwigs, Jellyby Child, Tomkins (Boy)**

Actor Six: plays **Miss Havisham, Kenwigs Child, Esther Summerson, Boy, Fanny Squeers**

The action of the play takes place on a bare stage
Time — nineteenth century

AUTHOR'S NOTE

Dickens, Actors Two and Four should be played by a man if possible; Actor Five should be a woman, and young, if possible. However, an ingenious director can cast fewer or more actors. Dickens, however, should always play the part of his child characters.

Actors switch roles very quickly and play many parts. They may take a small piece of costume – a shawl, or a hat, for example – to help change character. (There's no time for major changes.) The storytelling must flow without a break. Narrators remain on stage watching the relevant action. When characters "go" or "leave", they leave the action, not necessarily the stage.

The books featured are *Great Expectations, Nicholas Nickleby, Bleak House* and *David Copperfield.*

Nick Warburton

Other plays by Nick Warburton published by Samuel French Ltd

Distracted Globe
Domby-Dom
Don't Blame It on the Boots
The Droitwich Discovery
Easy Stages
Garlic and Lavender
Ghost Writer
The Loopshole
Melons at the Parsonage
Not Bobby
Receive This Light
Round the World with Class 6
Office Song
Sour Grapes and Ashes
Zartan

DICKENS' CHILDREN

A bare stage

On the stage there are: a couple of wooden chairs; a free-standing mirror-frame; and perhaps a coat rack or a bench holding props and costumes

When the play begins, only the central area is lit. Dickens is on stage, looking in the mirror as if preparing to go out

During the following, the rest of the cast emerges from the shadows

Dickens (*to the audience*) Some years ago, I went on a tour among some of the worst-lodged inhabitants of the old town of Edinburgh. In the closes and wynds of that picturesque place, I saw more poverty and sickness in an hour than many people would believe in a life.

In a room in one of these places, there lay, in an old egg-box which the mother had begged from a shop, a little feeble, wasted, wan, sick child. With his little wasted face and his little hot, worn hands folded over his breast, and his little bright, attentive eyes, I can see him now, as I have seen him for several years, look in steadily at me.

There he lay in his little frail box, which was not at all a bad emblem of the little body from which he was slowly parting — there he lay, quite quiet, quite patient, saying never a word. He seldom cried, the mother said; he seldom complained; he lay there, seeming to wonder what it was all about. God knows, I thought, as I stood looking at him, he had his reasons for wondering.

And to my mind he has been wondering about it ever since. Many a poor child, sick and neglected, I have seen since that time; many a poor sick child I have seen most affectionately and kindly tended by poor people, in an unwholesome house and under untoward circumstances, wherein its recovery was quite impossible; but at all such times I have seen my poor little drooping friend in his egg box, and he has always addressed his dumb speech to me, and I have always found him wondering what it meant, and why, in the name of a gracious God, such things should be!

The other actors gather round Dickens, looking at him

I have known a hundred like him. And when I go out to walk — which I do often and alone, and by night and over great distances — I seem to sense them with me. They are in the shadows, waiting to speak …

The other actors whisper lines from the scenes they're about to play. We might hear the voices of Magwitch, Miss Havisham, Barkis and so on

My dream children. And perhaps they are wretched and without hope, and perhaps they are celebrated and adored, but they are all, all bewildered by this strange world of adults, and they wonder at it. Just as I did when I was a child.

All but Actor Two — due to play Magwitch — and Dickens disperse into the shadows. As they go, the actors reset or turn over the chairs to represent gravestones

The Lights change. We are on the marshes in the dull light of dawn

I remember that the dark flat wilderness beyond the churchyard ——
One (*to the audience*)— with scattered cattle feeding on it, was the marshes; and that the low leaden line beyond, was the river; and

that the distant savage lair from which the wind was rushing was
the sea; and that the small bundle of shivers growing afraid of it
all and beginning to cry was …
Dickens (*to the audience*) Pip.

Dickens becomes Pip. He smiles shyly. Suddenly Magwitch —
Actor Two — leaps on him and pins him against a gravestone

Two Hold your noise! Keep still, you little devil, or I'll cut your
    throat!
Dickens (*to the audience*) A fearful man, all in coarse grey, with a
    great iron on his leg!
Three (*to the audience*) A man with no hat, and with broken shoes,
    and with an old rag tied round his head.
Four (*to the audience*) A man who had been soaked in water, and
    smothered in mud, and lamed by stones, and cut by flints, and
    stung by nettles and torn by briars.
Dickens (*as Pip*) Don't cut my throat, sir. Pray don't do it, sir.
Two Tell us your name! Quickly!
Dickens Pip, sir.
Two Once more. Give it mouth!
Dickens Pip. Pip, sir.
Two Show us where you live. Point out the place!

Dickens points it out. Actor Two grabs some (imaginary) bread
from Pip's hand, takes it aside and sits to devour it

    You young dog, what fat cheeks you ha' got.
Dickens (*to the audience; as Pip*) I believe they were fat, though
    I was at that time undersized for my years, and not strong.
Two Darn me if I couldn't eat 'em. And if I han't half a mind to!
Dickens (*to the audience; as Pip*) I earnestly expressed my hope
    that he wouldn't, and held tighter to the tombstone on which he
    had put me.
Two Now lookee here! Where's your mother?
Dickens (*as Pip*) There, sir!

Dickens points to a chair. Actor Two leaps up nervously

There, sir! Also Georgiana. That's my mother.

Two (*seeing that Dickens means the gravestone*) Oh! And is that your father alonger your mother?

Dickens Yes, sir; him too; late of this parish.

Two Ha! Who d'ye live with, supposin' you're kindly let to live, which I han't made up my mind about?

Dickens My sister, sir. Mrs Joe Gargery, wife of Joe Gargery, the blacksmith, sir.

Two Blacksmith, eh? (*He closes on Dickens and grabs him again*) Now lookee here, the question being whether you're to be let to live. You know what a file is?

Dickens Yes, sir.

Two And you know what wittles is?

Dickens Yes, sir.

Two You get me a file. And you get me wittles. You bring 'em both to me. Or I'll have your heart and liver out.

Dickens If you would kindly please to let me go, sir, perhaps I shouldn't be sick, and perhaps I could attend more.

Two You bring me, tomorrow morning early, that file and them wittles. You bring the lot to me. You do it, and you never dare to say a word and you shall be let to live. You fail and your heart and your liver shall be tore out, roasted and ate. Now, I ain't alone, as you may think I am. There's a young man hid with me, in comparison with which young man I am a angel. A boy may lock his door, may be warm in bed, may tuck himself up, may draw the clothes over his head, may think himself comfortable and safe, but that young man will softly creep and creep his way to him and tear him open. I find it very hard to hold that young man off of your insides. Now, what do you say?

Dickens (*to the audience; as Pip*) I said that I would get him the file, and I would get him what broken bits of food I could, and I would come to him early in the morning.

Two Say Lord strike you dead if you don't!

Dickens (*as Pip*) Lord strike me dead if I don't.

Two Now, you remember what you've undertook, and you remember that young man, and you get home!

Dickens Goo… good-night, sir. (*He moves away then turns back to watch*)
Three (*to the audience*) And he glanced about him over the cold wet flat.
Two I wish I was a frog. Or a eel!
Four (*to the audience*) At the same time, he hugged his shuddering body in both his arms and limped towards the low church wall, picking his way among the nettles, and among the brambles that bound the green mounds, as if he were eluding the hands of the dead people, stretching up cautiously out of their graves, to get a twist upon his ankle and pull him in.

Actor Two limps away

The Lights change. It's daylight again. Actors place the chairs together to suggest a door

Dickens (*to the audience; as Pip*) Ill-shapen and rough-tongued and so clearly poor — what does he intend towards me? I wonder at it, and can't ever be sure I'm right.
One (*to the audience*) But if they are rich or beautiful or grand?
Dickens (*to the audience; as Pip*) I still can't be sure. What do they want of me? What am I expected to do?

Actor Four, as Mr Pumblechook, steps forward

Four Pip!
Dickens (*as Pip*) Yes, Mr Pumblechook.
Four You are wanted. At Miss Havisham's. Come along, come along.

Dickens hurries over to Actor Four, who inspects him for tidiness

Miss Havisham is very grand. You understand, don't you? You're fortunate to be called for. You mustn't make an ass of yourself.

Dickens No, Mr Pumblechook.
Four This way.

Actor Four walks on and Dickens follows. During the following, they walk all the way round the stage until they come to the chairs

One (*to the audience*) Within a quarter of an hour they came to Miss Havisham's house, which was of old brick, and dismal, and had a great many iron bars to it. There was a courtyard in front, and that was barred; so, they had to wait, after ringing the bell, until someone should come to open it.

A bell rings. Actor Five, as Estella, steps forward to answer it

Five What name?
Four Pumblechook.
Five Quite right.
Four This is Pip.
Five This is Pip, is it? Come in, Pip.

Dickens steps into the house. Actor Four attempts to follow but Actor Five prevents him

Oh! Did you wish to see Miss Havisham?
Four If Miss Havisham wishes to see me.
Five Ah, but you see she don't.

Actor Five pushes Actor Four away. He retires, stung. Dickens looks round

Dickens The Manor House. Is that the name of this house, miss?
Five One of its names, boy.
Dickens It has more than one, then, miss?
Five One more. Its other name was Satis; which is Greek, or Latin, or Hebrew, or all three — or all one to me — for "enough".
Dickens Enough House; that's a curious name, miss.

Five Yes, but it meant more than it said. It meant that whoever had this house, could want nothing else. They must have been easily satisfied in those days, I should think. But don't loiter, boy.

Dickens and Actor Five walk round the stage during the following, taking a similar journey to the earlier one

The Lights dim

Three (*taking a lamp from the props rack; to the audience*) They went into the house by a side door and the first thing Pip noticed was that the passages were all dark, and that she had left a lamp burning there.

Actor Five passes Actor Three; Actor Three hands her the lamp

One (*to the audience*) She took it up, and they went through more passages and up a staircase, and still it was all dark, and only the lamp lighted them.

They stop by the door

Five Go in.
Dickens After you, miss.
Five Don't be ridiculous, boy; I'm not going in.

Actor Five walks away, taking the lamp with her. Six, with a white veil as Miss Havisham, steps forward and sits

Dickens (*to the audience; as Pip*) This was very uncomfortable, and I was half-afraid. However, the only thing to be done was to knock at the door, I knocked, and ——
Six Enter!

Dickens steps through the door and peers around without seeing Actor Six

Two (*to the audience*) It was a dressing-room. Prominent in it was a draped table with a gilded looking-glass, and what he made out at first sight to be a fine lady's dressing-table.

Six Who is it?

Two (*to the audience*) She was dressed in rich materials — satins, lace and silks — all of white. Her shoes were white. She had bridal flowers in her hair, but her hair was white.

One (*to the audience*) She had not quite finished dressing, for she had but one shoe on — the other was on the table near her hand — and her veil was but half-arranged.

Dickens (*to the audience; as Pip*) I saw that everything within my view which ought to be white, had been white long ago, and had lost its lustre, and was faded and yellow.

Three (*to the audience*) He saw that the bride within the bridal dress had withered like the dress and like the flowers, and had no brightness left but the brightness of her sunken eyes.

Six Who is it?

Dickens (*seeing her*) Pip, ma'am.

Six Pip?

Dickens Mr Pumblechook's boy, ma'am. Come — to play.

Six Come nearer; let me look at you. Come close.

Dickens nervously approaches Actor Six

Look at me. You are not afraid of a woman who has never seen the sun since you were born?

Dickens (*lying*) No.

Six (*putting her hand on her chest*) Do you know what I touch here?

Dickens Yes, ma'am.

Six What do I touch?

Dickens Your heart.

Six Broken! (*Pause*) I am tired. I want diversion, and I have done with men and women. Play.

Dickens looks round helplessly. He is at a loss

Dickens (*to the audience; as Pip*) She could hardly have directed an unfortunate boy to do anything in the wide world more difficult to be done under the circumstances.
Six I sometimes have sick fancies, and I have a sick fancy that I want to see some play. There. (*Pointing*) There! Play, play. Play!

Dickens makes a half-hearted attempt and stops. He hangs his head

Are you sullen and obstinate?
Dickens (*as Pip*) No, ma'am, I am very sorry for you, and very sorry I can't play just now. If you complain of me I shall get into trouble with my sister, so I would do it if I could; but it's so new here, and so strange, and so fine — and melancholy ...

Actor Six looks at Dickens and then at the mirror

Six So new to him, so old to me; so strange to him, so familiar to me; so melancholy to both of us! Call Estella. (*Pause*) Call Estella! You can do that. Call Estella. (*Impatiently*) At the door!
Dickens (*moving to the door; without conviction*) Estella!

Actor Five, as Estella, instantly appears. She sails past Dickens and goes to Actor Six

Six Let me see you play cards with this boy.
Five With this boy? Why, he is a common labouring boy!
Six Well? You can break his heart.
Five (*turning to Pip*) What do you play, boy?
Dickens Nothing but beggar my neighbour, miss.

Actor Five laughs

Six Beggar him.

Dickens and Actor Five kneel to mime playing cards while Actor Six watches

One (*to the audience*) So she sat, corpse-like, as they played at cards; the frillings and trimmings on her bridal dress looking like earthy paper.

Five He calls the knaves, Jacks, this boy! And what coarse hands he has! And what thick boots!

Three (*to the audience*) He'd never thought of being ashamed of his hands before; but he began to consider them a very indifferent pair.

Dickens (*to the audience; as Pip*) Her contempt for me was so strong, that it became infectious, and I caught it.

Five You're a stupid, clumsy labouring boy.

Six You say nothing of her. She says many hard things of you, but you say nothing of her. What do you think of her?

Dickens (*as Pip*) I don't like to say.

Six (*hobbling over to Dickens*) Tell me in my ear.

Dickens I think she is very proud.

Six Anything else?

Dickens I think she is very pretty.

Six Anything else?

Dickens I think she is very insulting.

Six Anything else?

Dickens I think I should like to go home.

Six And never see her again, though she is so pretty?

Dickens I am not sure that I shouldn't like to see her again, but I should like to go home now.

Six You shall go soon. (*Returning to her chair*) Play the game out.

Dickens (*to the audience; as Pip*) I played the game to an end with Estella, and she beggared me. She threw the cards down on the table when she had won them all, as if she despised them for having been won of me. (*He turns away, utterly humiliated*)

Two (*to the audience*) She gave him a triumphant glance in showing him out, as if she rejoiced that his hands were so coarse and his boots were so thick.

One (*to the audience*) Pip was passing out without looking at her, when she touched him with a taunting hand.

Five Why don't you cry?

Dickens (*as Pip*) Because I don't want to.
Five You do. You have been crying till you are half blind, and you
  are near crying now. (*She laughs*)

Actor Five pushes Dickens out of the room and hurries away

The Lights brighten again

Three (*to the audience*) And Pip went home, humiliated, ashamed,
  but — relieved to be going home.
Dickens (*to Actor Three*) Yes! Because home, you see, home is
  where he should be loved and cherished — and safe and admired.
  Yes, admired. Even beyond reason.
Three And there are such homes.
Dickens There are. I've seen them.

There is bustle as everyone arranges the stage for the Kenwigs

*Dickens and three of the narrators (Actors Two, Five and Six) will
become the Kenwigs' children*

Four (*to the audience*) It was the anniversary of that happy day on
  which the Church of England as by law established, had bestowed
  Mrs Kenwigs ——

One, as Mrs Kenwigs, comes forward

  — upon Mr Kenwigs, and in grateful commemoration of the
  same, Mrs Kenwigs had invited a few select friends to supper ...
Three (*to the audience*) Chief among whom was Mr Lillyvick, Mrs
  Kenwigs' uncle and a collector of the water rates.

Actor Three becomes Mr Lillyvick and sits comfortably

  The little Kenwigs, all girls and all with flaxen hair tied in
  luxuriant pigtails, were also allowed to attend.

The children, Dickens and Actors Two, Five and Six, smiling sweetly (and perhaps wearing pigtails), hurry forward and warm themselves by the imaginary fire

Four (*to the audience*) Everybody having eaten everything, the table was cleared in a most alarming hurry, and with great noise, and the party composed themselves for conviviality.

Three (*as Mr Lillyvick; to the audience*) Mr Lillyvick was stationed in a large armchair by the fireside, and the four little Kenwigses disposed on a small form with their faces to the fire; an arrangement which was no sooner perfected, than Mrs Kenwigs was overpowered by the feelings of a mother.

One (*as Mrs Kenwig*) They are so beautiful!

Four (*as Miss Petowker*) Oh, dear, so they are! It's very natural you should feel proud of that; but don't give way, don't.

One I cannot help it, and it don't signify; oh! They're too beautiful to live, much too beautiful!

Three (*as Mr Lillyvick; to the audience*) On hearing this alarming presentiment of their being doomed to an early death in the flower of their infancy, all four little girls ——

The children are struck with alarm. They scream and rush to their mother for comfort

—— and burying their heads in their mother's lap, screamed until the eight flaxen tails vibrated again.

During the following, the tearful children are escorted to seats to watch

Four (*as Miss Petowker; to the audience*) At length, the anxious mother permitted herself to be soothed into a more tranquil state, and the little Kenwigses, being also composed, were distributed among the company, to prevent the possibility of Mrs Kenwigs being again overcome with the blaze of their combined beauty.

One Morleena Kenwigs, kiss your dear uncle!

*One of the children (Actor Five) skips forward to kiss Mr Lillyvick
on the top of his head*

Four Oh dear, Mrs Kenwigs, do let Morleena go through that figure
dance before Mr Lillyvick.
One No, no, my dear. It will only worry my uncle.
Four It can't worry him, I am sure. You will be very much pleased,
won't you, sir?
Three That I am sure I shall.
One Well then, I'll tell you what, Morleena shall do the steps, if
uncle can persuade Miss Petowker to recite to us afterwards.

*There is a great clapping of hands and stamping of feet. Actor Four
pretends to be reluctant, though really she's pleased. Actor Five
comes c as Morleena and strikes a pose*

Three (*as Mr Lillyvick; to the audience*) The company being all
ready, Morleena danced a dance …

*Lively piano music plays — possibly the third movement of Schubert's
Piano Sonata in A Minor. Morleena whirls into a dance*

One (*as Mrs Kenwigs; to the audience*) It was a very beautiful
figure, comprising a great deal of work for the arms, and was
received with unbounded applause.

*Morleena strikes a finishing pose and the others clap. She skips back
to her place*

Four If I was blessed with a child of such genius as that, I would
have her out at the Opera instantly.
Three Miss Petowker was then entreated to begin …

*Pause. Actor Four stalks forward and prepares to chill their blood.
They all wait, pleasurably frightened*

Four The Blood Drinker's Burial!

The little Kenwigses scream and are all but frightened into fits. They rush to their mother for comfort. As they reach her, they stop being Kenwigs

Six (*to the audience*) Such fear and trepidation. But all quite safe, of course, within the bosom of a loving family. Is there a safer place for children to be? A mother devoted and a father doting.
Two Yes, there is.
Six Where?
Two The Jellybys.
Six Ah, the Jellybys.
Two (*indicating Actor Six*) Esther Summerson is to stay with Mrs Jellyby in London. (*Indicating Actor One*) Mrs Jellyby, as a notable family woman, is deemed to be the perfect hostess.

During the following, the chairs are rearranged to represent the Jellyby household. A change of lighting suggests the change of scene; the Jellyby house is colder than the Kenwigs'

Actor Six comes forward as Esther and Actor One as Mrs Jellyby. Mrs Jellyby sits and writes, discarding used sheets of paper on to the floor. Actor Three becomes Mr Kenge. The others gather at the back; they will become the Jellyby children

Three (*as Mr Kenge; to Actor Six*) Mrs Jellyby is a lady of very remarkable strength of character who devotes herself entirely to the public. She is at present devoted to the subject of Africa, with a view to the general cultivation of the coffee berry and the happy settlement, on the banks of the African rivers.
Six (*as Esther*) And Mr Jellyby, sir?
Three Ah! Mr Jellyby is — a ... I don't know that I can describe him to you better than by saying that he is the husband of Mrs Jellyby. I never, to my knowledge, had the pleasure of seeing Mr Jellyby. He may be a very superior man; but he is, so to speak, merged ... merged — in the more shining qualities of his wife.

Actor Four steps smartly forward as Mr Guppy. Actor Three turns and joins the children. In doing so, he becomes a child

Four (*as Mr Guppy*) I'll take you, miss; it's no distance. Only round the corner. We just twist up Chancery Lane, and cut along Holborn, and there we are in four minutes' time, as near as a toucher.

Actor Six and Actor Four set off on their walk

The children play; Actor Two gets his head stuck in some railings (a chair or the coat rack)

Six (*as Esther; to the audience*) There was a confused little crowd of people, principally children, gathered about the house at which we stopped.
Four Don't be frightened! One of the young Jellybys's been and got his head through the area railings!
Six (*as Esther*) O poor child!
Four Pray be careful of yourself, miss. The young Jellybys are always up to something.
Six (*as Esther; to the audience*) The poor child was one of the dirtiest little unfortunates I ever saw.

The children try to pull Actor Two out backwards. Mrs Jellyby continues writing and takes no notice

(*To the children*) As he is a little boy, with a naturally large head, perhaps where his head can go, his body might follow.
Five (*as a child*) How d'yer mean?
Six The best mode of extraction might be to push him forward.

The children push Actor Two forward, with much noise, and the child is released. Still talking, the children resume their play

Four (*to the audience*) We passed several more children on the way up, whom it was difficult to avoid treading on in the dark ...

One of the children yelps

(*To the child; as Mr Guppy*) Sorry. (*To the audience*) As we came into Mrs Jellyby's presence, one of the poor little things fell downstairs ...

We hear the child fall. They all remain still, waiting for the sound to finish

Six Down a whole flight it sounded to me.
Four (*clearing his throat*) Mrs Jellyby.

One, as Mrs Jellyby, stares vacantly into space and takes no notice

(*To the audience*) She was a pretty, very diminutive, plump woman of from forty to fifty, with handsome eyes, though they had a curious habit of seeming to look a long way off. As if they could see nothing nearer than Africa! (*To Mrs Jellyby; as Mr Guppy*) Mrs Jellyby!
One (*as Mrs Jellyby, getting up*) Ah!
Four Miss Esther Summerson to see you.

Actor Four goes

One I am very glad indeed to have the pleasure of receiving you. You find me, my dears, as usual, very busy. The African project at present employs my whole time. We hope by this time next year to have from a hundred and fifty to two hundred healthy families cultivating coffee and educating the natives of Borrioboola-Gha, on the left bank of the Niger.
Six That must be very gratifying.
One It is gratifying. Do you know, Miss Summerson, I almost wonder that you never turned your thoughts to Africa.
Six Well, the climate ...
One The finest climate in the world!
Six Indeed, ma'am?
One Certainly. With precaution. You may go into Holborn, without precaution, and be run over. You may go into Holborn, with precaution and never be run over. Just so with Africa.

One of the children enters. He's tearful and wants help. He kneels on one of Mrs Jellyby's discarded sheets. Mrs Jellyby spots him and hurls him cheerfully aside to retrieve her paper

No, Peepy! Not on my account!
Six (*as Esther; to the audience*) Peepy was the unfortunate child who had fallen downstairs, who now presented himself, with a strip of plaster on his forehead, to exhibit his wounded knees.
One (*brushing the child aside again*) Go along, you naughty Peepy! Six o'clock! And our dinner hour is nominally — for we dine at all hours — five!

Peepy attaches himself to Actor Six for some support

Oh, that very bad child! Pray put him down, Miss Summerson! (*She knocks him out of the way with a laugh*)

Everyone gathers round an imaginary table

Four (*to the audience, as Mr Guppy*) Soon after seven o'clock we sat down to dinner. We had a fine cod fish, a piece of roast beef, a dish of cutlets, and a pudding; an excellent dinner, if it had had any cooking to speak of, but it was almost raw.

Actor Three enters slowly and miserably as Mr Jellyby. The children stop eating and watch him curiously

Six (*as Esther; to the audience*) I was a little curious to know who a mild bald gentleman in spectacles was, who dropped into a vacant chair after the fish was taken away. It was not until we left the table, that the possibility of his being Mr Jellyby ever entered my head.
Four (*to the audience*) But he was Mr Jellyby.
Six During the whole evening, Mr Jellyby sat in a corner with his head against the wall as if he were subject to low spirits.
Dickens (*to the audience*) But, surely, it is a home. They all belong together.

During the following, the meal breaks up and two chairs are placed to form Barkis's cart

The Lights change: we are outside, in daylight. Actor Three sits, as Barkis

(*As David Copperfield*) When I was twelve I was sent away from home. You understand that, do you? I was put out to work. I was sent away from home! (*He cries as David and wipes his eyes on a handkerchief. He sits next to Barkis*)

Actor Three starts the cart

Two (*to the audience*) David Copperfield. They might have gone about half a mile, and David's pocket handkerchief was quite wet through, when the carrier stopped short ——

Actor Three stops the cart. Dickens is puzzled

— and Peggotty burst from a hedge.

One, as Peggotty, leaps forward and crushes Dickens in a hug. She gives him a bag of (imaginary) cakes and a purse of (imaginary) coins, then hugs him again and runs off, weeping. Actor Three is unmoved by this; making sure One's not about to come back, he starts the horse

Six (*to the audience*) David had now leisure to examine the purse. It had three bright shillings in it, which Peggotty had evidently polished with whitening, for his greater delight.
Four (*to the audience*) But its most precious contents were two half-crowns folded together in a bit of paper, on which was written, in his mother's hand …
Dickens (*reading*) "For Davy. With my love."

Dickens cries again. Actor Three is unmoved. Dickens recovers. They jog on in silence for a while

Dickens Are you going all the way?
Three All the way where?
Dickens There.
Three Where's there?
Dickens Near London.
Three Why that horse would be deader than pork afore he got over half the ground.
Dickens Are you only going to Yarmouth then?
Three That's about it. And there I shall take you to the stage cutch, and the stage cutch that'll take you to — wherever it is.
Six (*to the audience*) As this was a great deal for Mr Barkis to say — he being of a phlegmatic temperament, and not at all conversational — David offered him a cake as a mark of attention, which he ate at one gulp, exactly like an elephant.

Actor Three takes an imaginary cake and eats with appreciation

Three Did *she* make 'em, now?
Dickens Peggotty, do you mean, sir?
Three Ah! Her.
Dickens Yes. She makes all our pastry, and does all our cooking.
Three Do she though? (*He ponders*) No sweethearts, I believe?
Dickens Sweetmeats did you say, Mr Barkis?
Three Hearts. Sweethearts: no person walks with her!
Dickens (*amused*) With Peggotty?
Three Ah! Her.
Dickens Oh, no. She never had a sweetheart.
Three Didn't she, though! (*Pause*) So she makes all the apple pasties, and doos all the cooking, do she?
Dickens Yes.
Three Well. I'll tell you what. P'raps you might be writin' to her?
Dickens I shall certainly write to her.
Three Ah! (*Beat*) Well! If you was writing' to her, p'raps you'd recollect to say that Barkis is willin'; would you?
Dickens That Barkis is willing. Is that all the message?
Three Ye-es. Ye-es. Barkis is willin'.
Dickens But you will be at Blunderstone again tomorrow, Mr Barkis, and could give your own message so much better.

Three Barkis is willin'. That's the message.
Two Yarmouth! This is Yarmouth!

*Dickens and Actor Three get up. The Lights change. Actor Three
moves the chairs, setting them as if for a meal. There is bustle from
everyone*

One (*to Dickens*) Is that the little gentleman from Blunderstone?
Dickens Yes, ma'am.
One What name?
Dickens Copperfield, ma'am.
One William! Show him to the coffee room!

*Actor Three becomes a waiter. He dashes to Dickens, shows him to
a seat and places imaginary food before him*

Three (*as the waiter; affably*) Chops, and vegetables.

Dickens looks unhappy

  Now, six foot! Come on!

Actor Three watches intently as Dickens picks at his food

  There's half a pint of ale for you. Will you have it now?

Dickens Yes.

The waiter pours the imaginary ale

Three My eye! It seems a good deal, don't it?
Dickens It does seem a good deal.
Three There was a gentleman here, yesterday, a stout gentleman,
  by the name of Topsawyer — perhaps you know him?
Dickens No, I don't think so.
Three In breeches and gaiters, broad-brimmed hat, grey coat,
  speckled choker.

Dickens No, I haven't the pleasure …

Three He came in here, ordered a glass of ale — *would* order it — I told him not — drank it, and fell dead. It was too old for him. It oughtn't to be drawn; that's the fact.

Two (*to the audience*) David was very much shocked to hear of this melancholy accident.

Three Why you see, our people don't like things being ordered and left. It offends 'em. But I'll drink it, if you like. I'm used to it, and use is everything. I don't think it'll hurt me, if I throw my head back, and take it off quick. Shall I?

Dickens nods; Actor Three downs the drink

Six (*to the audience*) David had a horrible fear of seeing the waiter meet the fate of the lamented Mr Topsawyer, and fall lifeless on the carpet.

Actor Three totters for a moment, then laughs

Dickens (*as David Copperfield; to the audience*) But it didn't hurt him.

Six (*to the audience*) On the contrary, he seemed the fresher for it.

Three What have we got here? Not chops?

Dickens Chops.

Three Lord bless my soul! I didn't know they were chops. Why, a chop's the very thing to take off the bad effects of that beer! Ain't it lucky?

Actor Three sits down with Dickens and eats cheerfully

Four (*to the audience*) So he took a chop by the bone in one hand, and a potato in the other, and ate away with a very good appetite.

Two (*to the audience*) He afterwards took another chop, and another potato.

Six (*to the audience*) And after that, another chop and another potato.

Dickens (*as David Copperfield; to the audience*) I never saw anyone enjoy a chop so much, I think.

Actor Three leans back, replete

Three Where are you going to school?
Dickens Near London.
Three Oh, my eye! I am sorry for that.
Dickens Why?
Three Oh, Lord! That's the school where they broke the boy's ribs
     — two ribs … A little boy he was. I should say he was … Let me
     see — how old are you, about?
Dickens Between eight and nine.
Three That's just his age. He was eight years and six months old
     when they broke his first rib; eight years and eight months when
     they broke his second, and did for him.
Dickens How was it done?
Three With whopping.

Dickens jumps up in alarm. A distant coach horn is heard

Dickens Oh! That's my coach. I must … I have to …

The chairs are cleared away, preparing the stage for a street scene.
The Lights change. Actor Three retires into the shadows

Four (*handing Dickens a broom*) You don't see, do you? You don't
     see what he's up to.
Dickens (*as himself*) I see *now*, yes. But what's the use of that?
     Then, when all is bewilderment, you need someone to see for you.
Four You need the possibility of rescue. You need a champion.

Dickens, as Jo from Bleak House, sweeps. During the following, the
others cross and re-cross the road he's sweeping as they narrate

Dickens (*as Jo*) No-one to rescue Jo. Too far gone, too lost …
Two (*to the audience*) Jo sweeps his crossing all day long. He sums
     up his mental condition, when asked a question, by replying …
Dickens I don't know nothink.

Six (*to the audience*) He knows that it's hard to keep the mud off the crossing in dirty weather, and harder still to live by doing it. Nobody taught him, even that much; he found it out.

One (*to the audience*) Jo lives — that is to say, Jo has not yet died — in a ruinous place, known to the like of him by the name of Tom-all-Alone's. It is a black, dilapidated street, avoided by all decent people.

Three (*to the audience*) Now, these tumbling tenements contain, by night, a swarm of misery, a crowd of foul existence that crawls in and out of gaps in walls and boards; and coils itself to sleep, in maggot numbers, where the rain drips in.

Two (*to the audience*) It must be a strange state to be like Jo!

Five (*to the audience*) To see people read, and to see people write, and to see the postmen deliver letters, and not to have the least idea of all that language — to be, to every scrap of it, stone blind and dumb!

Six (*to the audience*) It must be very puzzling to see the good company going to the churches on Sundays, with their books in their hands, and to think what does it all mean, and if it means anything to anybody, how come that it means nothing to me?

Dickens (*to the audience; as Jo*) To be hustled, and jostled, and moved on; and to feel that I have no business here, or there, or anywhere

The cast stops crossing. Dickens sinks to his knees, weak and exhausted. The others gather round, but at a distance

One (*to the audience*) The day changes as it wears itself away, and becomes dark and drizzly. Twilight comes on; gas begins to start up in the shops; the lamplighter, with his ladder, runs along the margin of the pavement. A wretched evening is beginning to close in.

Dickens sleeps

Actor Six, as Esther, approaches Jo and tries to wake him. She fetches Actor Four, as Allan Woodcourt

Six (*to the audience*) Someone comes at last. But too late.

Three (*to the audience*) Jo is in a sleep or a stupor today, and Allan
    Woodcourt stands by him, looking down upon his wasted form.

Actor Four helps Dickens to sit up

Four (*as Allan Woodcourt*) Well, Jo. What is the matter? Don't be
    frightened.

Dickens I thought … I thought I was in Tom-all-Alone's agin. Ain't
    there nobody here but you, Mr Woodcot?

Four Nobody.

Dickens And I ain't took back to Tom-all-Alone's. Am I, sir?

Four No.

Dickens I'm wery thankful.

Four Jo! Did you ever know a prayer?

Dickens Never know'd nothink, sir.

Four Not so much as one short prayer?

Dickens No, sir. Nothink at all. Mr Chadbands he wos a-prayin'
    wunst at Mr Sangsby's and I heerd him, but he sounded as if he
    wos a-speakin' to his self, and not to me.

Two (*to the audience*) After a short relapse into sleep or stupor, he
    makes, of a sudden, a strong effort to get out of bed.

Four Stay, Jo! What now?

Dickens It's time for me to go to that there berrying ground, sir.

Four Lie down, and tell me. What burying ground, Jo?

Dickens Where they laid him as wos wery good to me. It's time fur
    me to go down to that there berryin' ground, sir, and ask to be put
    along with him. I wants to go there and be berried.

Four By and by, Jo. By and by.

Dickens Ah! P'raps they wouldn't do it if I wos to go myself. But
    will you promise to have me took there, sir, and laid along with
    him?

Four I will, indeed.

Dickens Thankee, sir. Thankee, sir. Is there any light a-comin'?

Four It is coming fast, Jo. Jo, can you say what I say?

Dickens I'll say anythink as you say, sir, for I knows it's good.

Four Our Father ——

Dickens Our Father! … Yes, that's wery good, sir.
Three — which art in heaven ——
Dickens Art in Heaven … Is the light a-comin', sir?
Four It is close at hand. Hallowed be thy name!
Dickens Hallowed be — thy ——

Pause

One (*to the audience*) The light is come upon the dark benighted way. Dead! Dead, your Majesty. Dead, my lords and gentlemen. Dead, Right Reverends and Wrong Reverends of every order. Dead, men and women, born with Heavenly compassion in your hearts. And dying thus around us, every day.
Six (*as Esther*) There must be someone, somewhere who will stand against this; who will at least speak against it.

Dickens stands to prepare for the next scene

Dickens (*touching Actor Four's shoulder*) Nicholas Nickleby.

Actor Four stands and steps forward, now as Nicholas. The others scatter and prepare the set for Dotheboys Hall; Actor Two fetches a cane and he and Actor One become Mr and Mrs Squeers; the others become boys. Dickens will become Smike

The Lights change

Five (*to the audience*) Nicholas Nickleby! His first morning at Dotheboys Hall.
Two (*as Mr Squeers; to the boys*) Look sharp, will you? (*To Actor Four*) It's brimstone morning, Nickleby. We purify the boy's bloods now and then.
One (*as Mrs Squeers*) Purify fiddlesticks' ends. They have the brimstone and treacle, partly because if they hadn't they'd be always ailing and giving a world of trouble, and partly because it spoils their appetites and comes cheaper than breakfast and dinner. So, it does them good and us good at the same time, and that's fair enough I'm sure. (*She stomps away*)

Two A most invaluable woman, that, Nickleby.

Four (*as Nicholas*) Indeed, sir!

Two I don't know her equal; I do not know her equal, Nickleby. To them boys she is a mother. But she is more than a mother to them; ten times more. She does things for them boys, Nickleby, that I don't believe half the mothers going would do for their own sons.

Four I should think they would not, sir.

Two But come, let's go to the schoolroom; and lend me a hand with my school coat, will you?

Actor Four helps Actor Two on with a jacket. They step into the schoolroom

There, this is our shop, Nickleby!

Actor Four stares, appalled. The narrators speak to the audience as boys

Five A bare and dirty room, with a couple of windows, whereof a tenth part might be of glass, the remainder being stopped up with old copybooks and paper.

Six A couple of long old rickety desks, cut and notched, and inked, and damaged, in every possible way.

Five The walls so stained and discoloured, that it was impossible to tell whether they had ever been touched with paint or whitewash.

Six But the pupils — the young noblemen! Children with the countenances of old men.

Three Little faces which should have been handsome, darkened with the scowl of sullen, dogged suffering.

Five Vicious-faced boys, brooding, with leaden eyes, like malefactors in a jail.

Four What an incipient Hell was breeding here!

One brings on a basin and spoon. The boys line up facing the back of the stage. One administers the brimstone and treacle

Three (*to the audience*) A row of boys waiting to be treacled.

The boys wince and turn round to face the front and form another line

Six (*to the audience*) And another file, who had just escaped from the infliction, making a variety of mouths indicative of anything but satisfaction.

Two Now! Is that physicking over?

One Just over. (*She taps a head with the spoon, wipes her hands on someone's hair*) Here, you Smike; take away now. Look sharp!

Dickens, as Smike, takes the basin from One and shuffles out

Two Right! To it, then! To it!

The boys stand to attention for lessons

This is the first class in English spelling and philosophy, Nickleby. We'll get up a Latin one, and hand that over to you. Now, then, where's the first boy?

Five (*as a boy*) Please, sir, he's cleaning the back parlour window.

Two So he is, to be sure. We go upon the practical mode of teaching, Nickleby; the regular education system. C-l-e-a-n, clean, verb active, to make bright, to scour. W-i-n, win, d-e-r, der, winder, a casement. When the boy knows this out of the book, he goes and does it. It's just the same principle as the use of the globes. Where's the second boy?

Three (*as a boy*) Please, sir, he's weeding the garden.

Two To be sure. So he is. B-o-t, bot, t-i-n, bottin, n-e-y, ney, bottinney, noun substantive, a knowledge of plants. When he has learned that bottinney means a knowledge of plants, he goes and knows 'em. That's our system, Nickleby; what do you think of it?

Four It's a very useful one, at any rate.

Two I believe you. Third boy, what's a horse?

Six (*as a boy*) A beast, sir.

Two So it is. Ain't it, Nickleby?

Four I believe there is no doubt of that, sir.

Two Of course there isn't. A horse is a quadruped, and quadruped's Latin for beast, as everybody that's gone through the grammar knows, or else where's the use of having grammars at all?

Four Where, indeed!

Two As you're perfect in that, go and look after my horse, and rub him down well, or I'll rub you down. The rest of the class go and draw water up, till somebody tells you to leave off, for it's washing day tomorrow, and they want the coppers filled.

Six (*to the audience*) So saying, he dismissed the first class to their experiments in practical philosophy.

The boys all shrink away

Two That's the way we do it, Nickleby. And a very good way it is, too. Now, just take them fourteen little boys and hear them some reading, because, you know, you must begin to be useful. Idling about here won't do.

Actors Two and One go

Four (*to the audience*) It was Mr Squeers' custom, in the afternoon of the day succeeding his return, to call the boys together, and make a sort of report, after every half-yearly visit to London, regarding the relations and friends he had seen, the news he had heard, the letters he had brought down, the bills which he had been paid, the accounts which had been left unpaid, and so forth.

Actor Two comes on again and someone hands him a bundle of letters. The boys line up; there's a murmur of excitement among them

Two Let any boy speak a word without leave, and I'll take the skin off his back! Boys, I've been to London, and have returned to my family and you, as strong and well as ever. (*He glares at the boys*)

The boys give three feeble cheers

I have seen the parents of some boys, and they're so glad to hear how their sons are getting on, that there's no prospect at all of their going away, which is a very pleasant thing to reflect upon, for all

parties. I have had disappointments to contend against; Bolder's father was two pound ten short. Where is Bolder?
Boys (*pointing into the audience*) Here he is, please sir.
Two Bolder, you're an incorrigible young scoundrel, and as the last thrashing did you no good, we must see what another will do towards beating it out of you. I'll see you after. (*Checking the letters*) Now let us see. A letter for Cobbey.

Actor Three steps forward hopefully

Cobbey's grandmother is dead, and his uncle John has took to drinking, which is all the news his sister sends, except eighteenpence, which will just pay for that broken square of glass. Mrs Squeers, my dear, will you take the money?

One comes on and takes the money from Actor Two. Actor Three, crestfallen, rejoins the line

Six (*to the audience*) Mr Squeers then proceeded to open a miscellaneous collection of letters; some enclosing money ——
One (*as Mrs Squeers; to the audience*) — which Mrs Squeers took care of ——
Five (*to the audience*) — and others referring to small articles of apparel, as caps and so forth, all of which the same lady stated to be ——
One — too large ——
Five (*to the audience*) — or ——
One — too small ——
Six (*to the audience*) — and calculated for nobody but young Squeers, who would appear to have most accommodating limbs, since everything that came into the school fitted him to a nicety.
Four (*as Nicholas; to the audience*) This business dispatched, a few slovenly lessons were performed, and Squeers retired to his fireside, leaving me to take care of the boys in the school room.

Actor Two and One go. The boys sit or curl up. Actor Four sinks into a chair

Three (*to the audience*) There was a small stove at that corner of the room and by it Nickleby sat down. The cruelty of which he had been an unwilling witness, the filthy place, the sights and sounds about him, all filled him with honest disgust and indignation.

Actor Four is lost in thought. Dickens, as Smike, creeps up to an imaginary fire suggested by a red glow

Four As I was absorbed in these meditations, I noticed Smike on his knees before the stove, picking a few stray cinders from the hearth and planting them on the fire. (*Pause. To Smike*) Smike.

Smike shrinks back, as if expecting a blow

You need not fear me. Are you cold?
Dickens N-n-o.
Four You are shivering.
Dickens I am not cold. I am used to it.
Four Poor fellow!

Nicholas fetches a cloak for Smike who begins to weep

Dickens Oh dear, oh dear! My heart will break. It will, it will. Do you remember the boy that died here?
Four What of him?
Dickens I was with him at night, and when it was all silent he cried no more for friends to come and sit with him, but began to see faces round his bed that came from home; he said they smiled, and talked to him; and he died at last lifting his head to kiss them. Do you hear?
Four Yes, yes.
Dickens What faces will smile on me when I die? Who will talk to me in those long nights?

A bell sounds

Four (*as Nicholas; to the audience*) The bell rang to bed: and the boy, subsiding at the sound into his usual listless state, crept away as if anxious to avoid notice.

Smike goes. The boys sleep

The Lights dip, then come up again without the glow of the fire

Three (*to the audience*) The cold, feeble dawn of a January morning was stealing in at the windows of the common sleeping room, when …
Four I looked upon the sleepers as a man would who missed something his eye was accustomed to meet, and had expected to rest upon. Smike?
Two (*off*) Now then, are you going to sleep all day up there?
One (*off*) You lazy hounds!
Four (*as Nicholas*) We shall be down directly, sir.
Two Down directly!

ActorsOne and Two come on

Ah, you'd better be down directly, or I'll be down upon some of you in less. Where's that Smike?
Four He is not here, sir.
Two Don't tell me a lie. He is.
Four He is not; don't tell me one.
Two We shall soon see that. I'll find him, I warrant you. (*He looks round*)

The boys cower

What does this mean? Where have you hid him?
Four I have seen nothing of him since last night.
Two Come, you won't save him this way. Where is he?
Four At the bottom of the nearest pond for aught I know.
Two Damn you, what do you mean by that? (*To all*) Where is he? Where?

Pause

Five (*as Tomkins*) Please, sir, I think Smike's run away, sir.
Two Ha! Who said that?

Boys (*pointing at Actor Five*) Tomkins, please sir.

Actor Two grabs Actor Five and brings him forward

Two So, you think he's run away, do you, sir?
Five (*as Tomkins*) Yes, please sir.
Two And what, sir, what reason have you to suppose that any boy would want to run away from this establishment? Eh, sir? (*He flings Actor Five aside*) Now if any other boy thinks Smike has run away, I shall be glad to have a talk with him. (*Pause*) Well, Nickleby. You think he has run away, I suppose?
Four I think it extremely likely.
Two Oh, you do, do you? Maybe you know he has?
Four I know nothing of the kind.
One (*to the boys*) Take pattern by Smike if you dare. See what he'll get for himself, when he is brought back; and, mind! I tell you that you shall have as bad, and twice as bad, if you so much as open your mouths about him.
Two If I catch him, I'll only stop short of flaying him alive. I give you notice, boys.
One *If* you catch him; you are sure to; you can't help it, if you go the right way to work. Go! Away with you!

Actors Two and One storm out

Six (*to the audience*) Nicholas remained behind, in a tumult of feeling, sensible that whatever might be the upshot of Smike's flight, nothing but painful and deplorable consequences were likely to ensue from it.
Four (*to the audience*) Death, from want and exposure to the weather, was the best that could be expected from the protracted wandering of so poor and helpless a creature. There was little, perhaps, to choose between this fate and a return to the tender mercies of the Yorkshire school.

The Lights dip. After a moment they come up again

Three (*to the audience*) Another day came, and Nicholas was scarcely awake when he heard the wheels of a chaise approaching the house. It stopped.

Dickens is thrown on by Actor Two and One

Two Lift him up!

A couple of boys move forward and lift Dickens up by his arms

Each boy keeps his place!

The boys leave Dickens and get into line

Nickleby! To your desk, sir. (*To Dickens*) Well? And have you anything to say for yourself?

No answer

Have you anything to say? (*Swishing the cane*) Stand a little out of the way, Mrs Squeers, my dear; I've hardly got room enough.
Dickens Spare me, sir!
Two Yes, I'll flog you within an inch of your life, and spare you that.
One Ha, ha, ha, that's a good 'un!
Dickens I was driven to do it.
Two Driven to do it, were you? Oh, it wasn't your fault; it was mine, I suppose — eh?
One (*cuffing Dickens*) A nasty, ungrateful, pig-headed, brutish, obstinate, sneaking dog. What does he mean by that?
Two Stand aside, my dear. We'll try and find out.

Pause. Actor Two hits a chair hard with his cane. Dickens calls out in pain, as if hit. The boys wince but daren't make a sound. Actor Two prepares to strike again

Four (*loudly*) Stop!

Two Who cried stop?
Four I. (*Stepping forward*) This must not go on.
Two Must not go on!
Four No! I say must not; shall not. I will prevent it.

Actor Two stares, stunned by this intervention

You have disregarded all my quiet interference in the miserable lad's behalf. Don't blame me for this public interference. You have brought it upon yourself, not I.
Two Sit down, beggar!
Four Wretch! Touch him at your peril! I will not stand by and see it done. My blood is up, and I have the strength of ten such men as you. Look to yourself, for by Heaven I will not spare you, if you drive me on!
Two Stand back.
Four I have a long series of insults to avenge, and my indignation is aggravated by the dastardly cruelties practised on helpless infancy in this foul den. Have a care; for if you do raise the devil within me, the consequences shall fall heavily upon your own head!

Actor Two cries out and hits the chair with the cane. Actor Four recoils as if hit. There's a horrified pause, then Actor Four turns on Actor Two and wrestles with him. As they struggle, the boys find their voices and begin to cheer Actor Four along. He grabs the cane and beats the other chair soundly

Yowling, Actor Two goes. Actor One jumps on Actor Four but the boys intervene and, shouting, drive her off. The boys leave. Dickens and Actor Four are left alone

Dickens Please, sir ... Please ...
Four Smike. What do you want?
Dickens To go with you, anywhere — everywhere. My kind friend, take me with you.

Four I am a friend who can do little for you ...
Dickens May I ... May I go with you?
Four Of course. You shall. And the world shall deal by you as it
does by me, till one or both of us shall quit it for a better. Come.

Actor Four leads Dickens out. Pause

Three (*to the audience*) I can see him now, as I have seen him
for several years ...

But Actor Six, as Fanny Squeers, steps forward

Six (*interrupting*) No. Just one moment. I won't have this ... (*She
brushes the narrators aside*)

Actor Five comes forward with pencil and paper

There's injustice here and I will not have it. I speak for my father,
since no-one else will.
Five (*to the audience*) Fanny Squeers.
Six (*snapping*) All right. They know. Take a letter.

Actor Five sits and writes

Dotheboys Hall, Thursday morning. Sir, my pa requests me to
write to you, the doctors considering it doubtful whether he will
ever recuvver the use of his legs which prevents his holding a pen.
We are in a state of mind beyond everything, and my pa is one
mask of brooses both blue and green. When he had done this to
my pa and jumped upon his body with his feet and also langwedge
which I will not pollewt my pen with describing, he assaulted my
ma with dreadful violence, dashed her to the earth, and drove her
back comb several inches into her head. A very little more and it
must have entered her skull. We have a medical certifiket that if
it had, the tortershell would have affected the brain. Me and my
brother were then the victims of his feury since which we have

suffered very much which leads us to the arrowing belief that we have received some injury in our insides, especially as no marks of violence are visible externally. I am screaming out loud all the time I write and so is my brother which takes off my attention rather and I hope will excuse mistakes. Hoping to hear from you when convenient, I remain, yours and cetrer, Fanny Squeers.

Actor Six stalks off, stops, and turns to come back as a narrator. Dickens reappears as himself

The Lights change. During the following, the others come on and collect what bits of costume or props remain in order to take them away when they exit

Dickens (*to the audience*) I meet her too, on my walks. And she was once a child, let me not forget. And Smike, and David, and Jo … And the little child I saw in the back streets of Edinburgh …

Three (*to the audience*) I can see him now, as I have seen him for several years, look in steadily at me. A little feeble, wasted, wan, sick child in an old egg box which the mother had begged from a shop …

Actor Three goes

Dickens With his little wasted face, and his little hot, worn hands folded over his breast, and his little bright, attentive eyes.

Six (*to the audience*) There he lay in his little frail box, which was not at all a bad emblem of his little body from which he was slowly parting — there he lay, quite quiet, quite patient, saying never a word.

Actor Six goes

Two (*to the audience*) He seldom cried, the mother said; he seldom complained; he lay there, seeming to wonder what it was all about. God knows, I thought as I stood looking at him, he had his reasons for wondering.

Five (*to the audience*) And to my mind he has been wondering about it ever since.

Actor Two and Actor Five go

Four (*to the audience*) Many a poor child, sick and neglected, I have seen since that time; many a poor sick child I have seen most affectionately and kindly tended by poor people, in an unwholesome house and under untoward circumstances, wherein its recovery was quite impossible.

Actor Four goes

One (*to the audience*) But at all such times I have seen my poor little drooping friend in his egg box, and he has always addressed his dumb speech to me …

Actor One goes. Dickens is left alone

Dickens And I have always found him wondering what it meant, and why, in the name of a gracious God, such things should still be!

The Lights fade. Music plays

FURNITURE AND PROPERTY LIST

On stage: Two wooden chairs
Free-standing mirror frame
Coat rack or bench. *On it*: lamp for **Three**; correspondence and papers for **One**; bag and purse for **One**; broom for **Four**; cane for **Two**; basin and spoon for **One**; bundle of letters for **Two**; pencil and paper for **Five**

Personal: **Barkis**: handkerchief

LIGHTING PLOT

Practical fittings required: nil
A bare stage

To open: Central area of stage lit

Cue 1	The actors reset the chairs *Change lights to dull dawn setting*	(Page 2)
Cue 2	**Actor Two** limps away *Change lights to daylight setting*	(Page 5)
Cue 3	**Dickens** and **Actor Five** walk round the stage *Dim lights*	(Page 7)
Cue 4	**Actor Three** hands **Actor Five** a lamp *Brighten lights slightly*	(Page 7)
Cue 5	**Actor Five** walks away with the lamp *Dim lights to Cue 3 state*	(Page 7)
Cue 6	**Actor Five** pushes **Dickens** out and hurries away *Brighten lights*	(Page 11)
Cue 7	Chairs are rearranged *Change lighting to colder setting*	(Page 14)
Cue 8	Chairs are placed to form **Barkis**'s cart *Change lights to daylight setting*	(Page 18)
Cue 9	**Actor Two**: "Yarmouth! This is Yarmouth!" *Lights change to coffee room setting*	(Page 20)
Cue 10	**Dickens**: "I must ... I have to..." *Change lights to street setting*	(Page 22)

Cue 11   Set is prepared for Dotheboys Hall   (Page 25)
           Change lights to school interior setting

Cue 12   **Smike** creeps up to imaginary fire   (Page 30)
           Bring up red fireglow effect

Cue 13   **Smike** goes.The boys sleep   (Page 31)
           Dip lights, then return to Cue 11 setting

Cue 14   **Four**: " … mercies of the Yorkshire school."   (Page 32)
           Dip lights, then return to Cue 13 setting

Cue 15   **Dickens** returns   (Page 36)
           Change lights to general setting

Cue 16   **Dickens**: " … such things should still be!"   (Page 37)
           Fade to black-out

EFFECTS PLOT

Cue 1   **One**: " … come to open it."   (Page 6)
Bell rings

Cue 2   **Three**: "Morleena danced a dance ..."   (Page 13)
Music — possibly the third movement of
Schubert's Piano Sonata in A Minor

Cue 3   **Four**: " … poor little things fell downstairs …"   (Page 16)
Sound of several objects — pots and pans — falling,
ending with "Ouch!"

Cue 4   **Dickens** jumps up in alarm   (Page 22)
Distant coach horn

Cue 5   **Dickens**: " ... talk to me in those long nights?"   (Page 30)
Bell rings

Cue 6   The Lights fade   (Page 37)
Music

Printed by The Kingfisher Press, London NW10 7AS

9 780573 023743